Dog Woman

Helen Quah

Out-Spoken Press
London

Published by Out-Spoken Press,
Unit 39, Containerville
1 Emma Street
London, E2 9FP

All rights reserved
© Helen Quah

The rights of Helen Quah to be identified as the author of this work have
been asserted by them in accordance with section 77 of the Copyright,
Designs and Patents Act 1988.

A CIP record for this title is available from the British Library.

This book is in copyright. Subject to statutory exception and to provisions
of relevant collective licensing agreements, no reproduction of any part
may take place without the written permission of Out-Spoken Press.

First edition published 2022
ISBN: 978-1-8384272-6-9

Typeset in Adobe Caslon
Design by Patricia Ferguson
Printed and bound by Print Resources

Out-Spoken Press is supported using public funding by the National
Lottery through Arts Council England.

'My body is estrangement'
— Li-Young Lee

For my family

Contents

Like Deers We Eat

Metal doors open
onto an empty
driveway we've held
hands for too long
like deers we eat
from the lowest
branches
tighten then
unscrewing
our stomachs
filled with wild berries
ground up
excellence
when I rest my head
on your hip's verge, mother
I can hear
the nerves
and great vessels
arch and skip
through the inlets
of bone like
reaching
which you would
say is the most
important
of gestures

Suburbia

Women are auditioning
to be themselves.
They practice reciting
their lines with terrible
conviction
in back bedrooms
inside fitted wardrobes.
Even a smile can be a knot.

*

Women are on the TV mute
dry coughing into their hands.
Sat in plazas stale as Bundt cake.
Women find other women's
voices garish and loud.
The laughter perverse.
Instead of talking today
to a loved one, they prefer
to watch white noise.
Silent horses with arthritic pain.

*

Women are sailing large boats
too big to jump off.
The waves fall logically.
Before the sun develops
on film they all will have been
caught, shelled, and sorted
by their respective hair types.

*

Dragging handbags up the street
scuffing silk bottoms on the ground.
Sometimes followed by their dogs.
Sometimes followed by their husbands.
Wearing their beliefs like a waistcoat
tight around the midriff.
We all have shit to carry.

*

Women are counting cigarettes.
One for each man running
the perimeter gently rumbling
in their jeeps.
The open road is salvageable
they say to the fifth
before lighting its soggy end.

*

Women in the discotheque.
Women on the autobahn.
It's believed the inside of a woman's thigh
is longer than a piece of Sellotape.
The grip of a woman's hand
can hold a child's, a man's,
a woman's and crush them all.

Women can make the same sound
as a wolf and they do.

[When I Marry A White Man] II

When we enter our hotel room
my husband puts the receiver
on the table and keeps his shoes on.
The room smells burnt like carpet
has the stale colours of old sitcoms.
Beneath the sink are naked shelves,
a mouse's dying wish, antidote,
memory of monotonous father
carving in the garden. I hear
the TV switch off. 'Come to bed.'
With his arm up behind
his head, I fuck my husband.
He hopes our daughter
will inherit my good will.
My dainty feet and strong legs.

We Don't Look For Comfort

I am made completely
of empty promises
my sister of forest fires
        hydrogen bonds
        birthday cake
        we love
syrup because it has been
made for us
we are polite young women
swallowing the yellow earth
fungus in the shower curtain
once two men mistook
us for masseuses
in an alleyway in Soho
            we were eleven and fifteen
I still rub my belly
when in distress
we have entered
each new crisis together
as we age the air around our bodies
swells to a darker jade
        we take off our feet
unclipped at the ankle
our heels land three inches
           from the finish line

The Sentiment

was clear as crab cake
You whistled through my mouth
The sound cold
like a radiator
settled at the bottom of a lake
We volunteered to go last in the queue
You put my name down on the pink slip
You scoffed
I cramped
Peeled orange rind from between my legs
You made soup that digested
I was an alimentary canal
The tobacco stained your soul
My beautiful boy
I tucked you away in front of my telly
The only way to love
like big coats
covering the details

You Saw a White Woman Selling Islamic Prayer Mats as Gifts

                              how
she would even call to Him

everyone sounds the same
talking to God or their Mother

God, Mother. Each name
an engine running on memory

and doused in chicken fat
at the dinner table

they both fit neatly between
your hands: as charms or fruit flies

you see the land of God
and Mothers as symmetrical

you visit their kingdoms once
every springtime when the clocks

have either moved forwards
or tell you to go back

the weather has grown
the sun a giant toddler

tumbling across your shoulders
then the wind

Popsicles

We take our clothes off in the bathroom
hair knotted through the shower curtain
you wore a work jacket the insignia
of two golden snakes; a tired but sinister
ring wrapped around your genitals
and there is a slice of metal in the air
our tongues clinging to themselves
until you light a cigarette
the ash warrants goose bumps
and I let you tie my hands behind my head
the cramp in my stomach beginning to sing
we're so far away from being children
but we keep whispering anyway

[When I Marry A White Man] III

I'm made of stains and hiccups.
There are old honeymoon photos
sunk into the top shelf of our marriage.
We stood on the same bridge
my father took my mother
to catch the fattest butterflies.
Grasping our stringy nets,
I expected the re-enactment
to be stunning, but my husband
was threatened by the dirt of the place
and the sweat and sun cream
poured into his eyes like traffic.
I'm left with the image
of a dog in pain.

Self

Right now
my cousin is learning
the quiet of his mother
a four-toned climate
mosquitoes crave his knees fleshy
loving before he's thought about it
I sometimes want to know what it feels like to be white
    I sometimes have a pretty good idea
       then a van turns the corner all over my dress
         my head dilating
            in the rear-view mirror

Fifteen Minutes

After Kim Hyesoon

One day she'll be dead. She'll want to come and meet you on the driveway. Arriving fifteen minutes before you are quite ready. Come. Come. She will tell you to wash your hair. Ants will make a home beneath the ground where she used to warm her feet.

One day she will embrace you like you've stepped through a shared door together. Stroke your ripened cheeks with approval. Proceed to put the oven on too high. You will fight with her like in life. You will quarrel with the slugs that eat her variegated plants. The pathy holes in them will seem vast and seismic and spiritual.

Look at the greying follicles on her head. Thank the blackbirds that you don't need to worry about her hair falling out anymore. The dead leaving the dead is not something that troubles you.

Dead Mother will want to eat early. Take drugs with you. Do her nails with you. Express some milk with you. Your breasts ache as she sits downstairs alone, laughing with the television.

Dog Woman

After Paula Rego

The artist came out howling
and never stopped.
There are her memories.
There are her muscular women.
Beaten back hair. Kinetic jaws.
Watch out for their ruin!
They howl too, flicking ticks
from their rumps. Dresses
flung up. They can hold
and cut and salvage
as well as dance.
Their backs tremendous bows.
O and their knees are glorious!
They ride horses, eat lettuce,
have abortions on leather sofas,
cradling soft toys in their groins.
They wear fear's dark oil
to keep warm.
Sleep as peacefully as dogs
tucked up on their owners' coats.

Hungry Little Swamps

We owed the man on the corner three piglets.
You'd told him we'd have the last by early next week.
You smoked until the windows laughed
and your sides kept splitting and splitting
        into hungry little swamps.
I never cooked but my elbows felt
like meat cleavers.
My slatherings of potato grease.
I lay down naked waiting for the unaltered moon.
Attempted to imitate the squeal.

Skin Teeth Na Laugh

For Lucille

standing by her tomb
I watch the crickets mutter

pecking at necks like pieces of dried corn
she would have scolded me for scratching

the corner where my lips take root
rubbing my shoes into the earth like that

in her eighties she was sweeping dirt
an attempt to levitate

wearing a cross that read:
'In Good Times We Function'

as if her daughter had never left
now she is trying to lift

her stone
like the hem of a dress

the wind is wide behind me
bits of old speech find my body

we learn love from our mothers
turning softly, softly

[When I Marry A White Man] IV

The babies have learnt
to hurt like him.
I sometimes think
they laugh at his jokes
more than mine.
Reading one sense
in my arms and another in his.
When the house is quiet
and I've emptied all kindness
from its fact — I'll touch a face
in the wet mirror. Pour over
my worn slab half myself awake
more brutal than before.

Luxury Rabbits

The rabbits over there
munching on carrot
leaves
and figs
luxurious rabbits
skin sewn by the gods
I am told
they have always had
much more than us —
who equates want with life?
      unravel me in a church
and I will think of you
when I am riding out of sleep
on a pink wave
what the neuroscientist would call
the 'hypnopompic state'
fall for me and I will kill
the rabbits who
are jumping
up and down now
sensing closure
bundles of stuffed
ribbon not rigorously
just as much
as they need
to get past
the gate

Acknowledgements

Incredibly grateful to the Out-Spoken Press team, Patricia, for their wonderful support in making this book. With special thanks to Wayne and Anthony for giving me the confidence in this work, for their insight and kindness.

Thanks and love to my beautiful friends.

Forever grateful to my mum, dad and Grace for everything I have to be proud of.

Other titles by Out-Spoken Press

Caviar • SARAH FLETCHER

Somewhere Something is Burning • ALICE FRECKNALL

flinch & air • LAURA JANE LEE

Fetch Your Mother's Heart • LISA LUXX

Seder • ADAM KAMMERLING

54 Questions for the Man Who Sold a Shotgun to My Father
JOE CARRICK-VARTY

Lasagne • WAYNE HOLLOWAY-SMITH

Mutton Rolls • ARJI MANUELPILLAI

Contains Mild Peril • FRAN LOCK

Epiphaneia • RICHARD GEORGES

Stage Invasion: Poetry & the Spoken Word Renaissance
PETE BEARDER

Nascent • VOL 1: AN ANTHOLOGY

Ways of Coping • OLLIE O'NEILL

The Neighbourhood • HANNAH LOWE

The Games • HARRY JOSEPHINE GILES

Songs My Enemy Taught Me • JOELLE TAYLOR

To Sweeten Bitter • RAYMOND ANTROBUS

Dogtooth • FRAN LOCK

How You Might Know Me • SABRINA MAHFOUZ

Heterogeneous, New & Selected Poems
ANTHONY ANAXAGOROU

Titanic • BRIDGET MINAMORE

Email: press@outspokenldn.com